Joel

GETTING REAL WITH GOD

CWR

Steve Bishop

Contents

Introduction

'Get real!' This instruction might be applicable for those of us who are inclined to act first and think afterwards. Or it might be used to shock someone easily swayed by false impressions or misguided ideas. The world through which we navigate is abounding with data, possibilities, suggestions and options. Technology means that our senses can be significantly influenced by the continual bombardment of information wherever we are and whatever we might be doing. So there is a distinct need for all of us to guard against 'unreality'.

It's not just the internet that might be to blame for our unrealistic attitudes and expectations. It seems that our minds are wired to constantly engage in thinking, processing, imagining and projecting from all the multiple sources that surround us. So we all need to double check what we take onboard and subsequently process. The areas of life where this might apply are hugely varied and wide ranging. It might include entertaining the possibility of your football team winning a match against higher ranked opposition. (Such hopes are never held for long with my local team!) It might mean hoping that a short-cut through a major city will get you to your destination quicker, only to be hampered by no-entry signs and one-way systems. Or you might be tempted by adverts that claim to sort out problems, until reading the words 'terms and conditions apply' brings a reality check.

God's message
The necessity to 'Get real!' is not just applicable to twenty-first-century life. The Bible records God expressing a similar sentiment to His chosen people. And they were not words that they heard on just one occasion. God repeatedly urged His people to 'Get real!' because they frequently pushed Him out of their lives. In His place, they allowed, or were attracted towards, alternative possibilities – except these alternatives

weren't real or helpful, and God's people regularly got themselves into dire situations.

The history of the Israelites constantly featured times when they took their spiritual eyes off God and focused on unreal alternatives. Their miraculous escape from Egypt didn't positively impact them for long. They soon started grumbling: 'If only we had died by the LORD's hand in Egypt! There we sat round pots of meat and ate all the food we wanted, but you [Moses] have brought us out into this desert to starve this entire assembly to death' (Exod. 16:3). God's subsequent provision of food, water and protection in the barren desert for 40 years didn't make them grateful to Him either. When spies brought back a negative report about the Promised Land, they responded: 'Why is the LORD bringing us to this land only to let us fall by the sword? Our wives and children will be taken as plunder. Wouldn't it be better for us to go back to Egypt?' (Num. 14:3).

Serious consequences
Despite their negativity, God's miraculous intervention secured the Israelites the land that He had promised them. But it didn't stop their self-willed attitude. After Joshua and the subsequent elders died, we then read: 'the Israelites did evil in the eyes of the LORD and served the Baals. They forsook the LORD, the God of their ancestors, who had brought them out of Egypt. They followed and worshipped various gods of the peoples around them. They aroused the LORD's anger' (Judg. 2:11–13).

A succession of judges were sent by God to deliver His people from their enemies whom He had allowed to afflict, but only after the Israelites 'got real' and repented. However, their ongoing tendency to wander away from God soon returned. Eventually, the kingdom of Israel (as it had become under the kingship of Saul, David and Solomon) fragmented into two separate nations. The northern tribes (under the name 'Israel') set up their own monarchy and system of worship. Despite the call of God to 'get real' regarding their idolatry and its abhorrent outworking, the people refused to turn back. There were serious consequences: He subsequently allowed them to suffer complete disintegration, overrun by the forces of the Assyrian empire.

Sadly, the fate of their compatriots failed to have any lasting impact on the remaining people of God in the southern kingdom of Judah. But, as had been the case with the northern kingdom, God continued to send His messengers – prophets – to warn them of the need to 'get real' and turn back to Him.

Personally relevant
Commentators are uncertain as to where the prophet Joel actually appeared in the historical timeline of the Israelite people. Joel's message from God could have been applicable at various points in Jewish history – but it's also relevant to ourselves. Although our surroundings and lifestyles are totally different from those Jews of centuries ago, we share with them the same tendency to wander away from God, believing that other attractions can bring satisfaction. God needs to say the same to us: 'Get real!' The implications of that direct message are worked out as we consider Joel's prophecy. Are we ready to 'get real' about ourselves and God?

WEEK ONE

Realisation

Opening Icebreaker

Read and compare the front page headlines from a selection of current newspapers (either local or national). What is their focus and how accurately do they refer to the subsequent report?

Bible Readings

- Joel 1:1–12
- 2 Samuel 24:1–16
- 1 Kings 17:1
- 2 Chronicles 6:26–31
- Psalm 105:23–38

Opening Our Eyes

Was Joel a journalist? He was clearly a prophet sent by God, and the 'son of Pethuel' (Joel 1:1). His name alone constituted a necessary reminder as 'Joel' meant 'The LORD is God.' But as nothing else is known about him, other details are open to conjecture. However, he did have a way with words. The opening of his prophecy didn't pull any punches. His aim was like that of a modern-day journalist whose banner headline, 'Unprecedented Disaster', is designed to grab the attention of potential readers. Joel clearly identified his audience: 'Hear this, you elders; listen, all who live in the land.' He then went for a full-blown attention-getter: 'Has anything like this ever happened in your days or in the days of your ancestors?' (Joel 1:2).

Joel's words were designed to shock. They were directed at God's people, the Jews. Although a chosen and special people, they were not exempt from the effects of turning their backs on Him. Essentially it was not Joel who was needing to attract their attention, but God. And the means He was doing so was being underlined in big, bold 'print' by the prophet.

Devastation

The event to which Joel was drawing attention was something that our contemporary media would term a 'natural disaster'. The prophet was reporting on a swarm of locusts sweeping through the country. It's reckoned that such a swarm could consist of up to 600 million grasshopper-sized insects covering around 400 square miles and eating up to 80,000 tons of whatever consumables lay in their path per day. For the agriculturally dependent economy of that time, those effects were totally devastating. Perhaps a modern-day comparison would be a complete collapse (through overload or malicious hacking) of our national computer systems. Such a failure would have mind-blowing repercussions.

Joel's description, likening those locusts to an invading army (v6), would affect everyone. He lists those who would sustain irreparable loss – drinkers of wine, priests, farmers and vine growers. In fact, Joel sums it up by including everyone: 'Surely the people's joy is withered away' (v12).

Grabbing attention
But why is Joel going to such lengths – and adopting this journalistic style – to state the obvious? He was not aiming to increase the circulation of his newspaper, or 'hits' on his website! His words constituted a wake-up call. The people of God needed to face up to the reality of what was happening. They needed to realise that those locusts were not actually a natural disaster, a result of the greenhouse effect, the consequence of deforestation or lack of ecological awareness. The unprecedented nature of what they were experiencing should have made the Jews alert to the need to stop *and* think. It had certainly made them stop. But they had failed to think through the possible underlying reasons for this calamity. So, 'The word of the LORD that came to Joel' (v1) was God's means of addressing this failure. He was grabbing their attention in order for them to 'get real' about their spiritual condition. Having got their attention, God could now say important things to them through His prophet, Joel.

Discussion Starters

1. What were the devastating effects caused by the swarm of locusts, as described by Joel? Why do you think such detail was needed?

2. Why did Joel liken the locusts to an invading army? How is that relevant when considering natural disasters?

3. What were the different ways that Joel instructed the people to respond to this calamity? What would those reactions indicate?

4. Why do you think that Joel initially addressed his prophecy to 'the elders' (v2)? How might this particularly apply to our contemporary church life?

5. What other natural disasters, described in the Bible, are sent by God? (See 2 Sam. 24:1–16; 1 Kings 17:1; 2 Chron. 6:26–31; Psa. 105:23–38.)

_____

_____

_____

_____

6. What are the differences between manmade and natural disasters, as indicated in the media? How do those differences affect our reactions to them?

_____

_____

_____

_____

7. Why didn't God's people realise who was behind the invasion of locusts at first? In what ways can we be similarly oblivious to God speaking to us?

_____

_____

_____

_____

8. How can we be more alert to the different ways that God intervenes in the affairs of the world?

_____

_____

_____

_____

Personal Application

The starting point of Joel's prophecy was to draw attention to the fact that God was active in *all* the affairs of the world. Events that we might label as 'natural disasters' should make us realise that humankind cannot control everything that takes place on this planet. They also particularly point us to God who, as Scripture clearly shows, can make use of such calamities to awaken people from their disregard of Him. The particular force of those 'natural disasters' arises when they clearly threaten or affect our personal lives, perhaps in terms of our livelihood, lifestyle or health. It's at that point where we are brought to 'get real' about God demanding our attention.

Seeing Jesus in the Scriptures

Jesus' teaching frequently pointed to situations and events that showed God at work. His use of questions as a means of teaching His followers was a particularly probing 'tool'. Following His calming of a seriously fierce storm – a very 'natural' event – Jesus asked His disciples, 'Why are you so afraid?' (Mark 4:40). They needed to realise that He was with them in the storm – they should not have disregarded His presence – and had power over that threatening situation, which they had viewed as overwhelming. Jesus' follow-up question was also pointed: 'Do you still have no faith?' The disciples needed to realise that there was a greater 'reality' than the physical power of that storm.

WEEK TWO

Repentance

Opening Icebreaker

Reflect on a minor domestic problem that you've recently encountered, such as misplacing door keys or receiving an unexpectedly large energy bill. What questions were asked to resolve that situation?

Bible Readings

- Joel 1:13–20
- 1 Kings 21:20–29
- Nehemiah 1:1–11
- Daniel 9:1–11
- Jonah 3:3–10
- Mark 1:1–15

Opening Our Eyes

Airliners landing at major airports are a common sight. But
when a British Airways Boeing approached London Heathrow
in January 2008, a sudden emergency arose. Both engines
had lost all power. Skilful handling by the pilots prevented
a catastrophic crash and the airliner landed safely (but
heavily) on the runway threshold. Questions were naturally
asked. What happened? Why did it happen? Who was to
blame? Investigations revealed that ice had blocked the fuel
system; engine designers had failed to factor in this remote
possibility. Fortunately no one was seriously injured, but
where crashes have sadly resulted in fatalities, detailed
enquiries are undertaken to prevent recurrence. However,
asking probing questions when 'natural', rather than
'manmade', disasters occur is not so straightforward.

What? Why? Who?

When Joel appeared on the scene following the devastating
invasion of locusts, he brought, 'The word of the LORD' (v1)
into the situation. He was able to answer the 'what', 'why' and
'who' questions. It clearly underlined what had taken place.
'Has not the food been cut off from before our very eyes...
The storehouses are in ruins, the granaries have been broken
down, for the grain has dried up' (Joel 1:16–17). There is an
indication that a drought had followed those locusts: 'the
streams of water have dried up' (v20).

God's prophet had answered the 'What happened' question.
Joel also indicated why it had happened and who was
responsible. God wanted the attention of His people who had
failed to follow Him. Although the precise nature of what they
had done is not described, the action now needed (initially by
the priests and elders) was clearly spelt out: God's people were
directed to 'get real' and repent before Him.

Not unexpected

God's instruction to His people to repent shouldn't have
been unexpected; King Solomon had already described the
appropriate response to sin. Years previously, his prayer of
dedication focused on a scenario that Joel's contemporaries
were now experiencing. 'When the heavens are shut up and
there is no rain because your people have sinned against you,
and when they pray... and turn from their sin because you
have afflicted them... When famine or plague comes... locusts
or grasshoppers... when a prayer or plea is made... then hear
from heaven... Forgive, and deal with everyone according to
all they do... so that they will fear you and walk in obedience
to you all the time' (2 Chron. 6:26–31).

Joel's description of mourning, wailing, declaring a fast,
calling an assembly and crying out to God were all pointing to
one thing: the need to repent (Joel 1:12–14). Wearing sackcloth
(a coarse, unfinished material) was an outward sign of
penitence for actions and attitude contrary to God. The King of
Nineveh had decreed that this practice be undertaken by every
person (and beast) in the city in response to God's message of
judgment through the prophet Jonah (Jonah 3:3–10). Even evil
King Ahab responded to God's word through Elijah by putting
on sackcloth and fasting (1 Kings 21:27). Fasting was a similar
outward act showing an inner change of heart and mind in
terms of turning back to God (Neh. 1:4; Dan. 9:3).

A warning

The instruction from Joel included a warning. 'For the day
of the LORD is near' (Joel 1:15). The Israelite people not only
needed to 'get real' about their waywardness underlined by
their present plight, but also on account of what God was
yet to do.

Discussion Starters

1. Why do you think that Joel's call for acts of repentance was initially to the priests?

    _____

    _____

    _____

    _____

2. Why was God listing those outwards acts of repentance, including those to be undertaken at night-time? How does this relate to us?

    _____

    _____

    _____

    _____

3. Why do you feel that Joel repeated details of the locust invasion and the drought after the call to repent?

    _____

    _____

    _____

    _____

4. What were the elders (v14) and Joel (v19) actually to call out to God (see Neh. 1:4–11; Dan. 9:1–11)?

    _____

    _____

    _____

    _____

5. What do the accounts of King Ahab (1 Kings 21:20–29) and the King of Nineveh (Jonah 3:3–10) show us about God's response to repentance?

_____

_____

_____

_____

6. In what way was repentance integral to the ministry of John the Baptist and how does this link up with Joel's role (see Mark1:1–8)?

_____

_____

_____

_____

7. In what ways did Jesus validate John the Baptist's message about the need for repentance?

_____

_____

_____

_____

8. Has the Church today toned down the need to repent? How can it emphasise afresh (or maintain) this vital aspect of coming to God?

_____

_____

_____

_____

Personal Application

Repentance involves a deliberate humbling before God, acknowledging and confessing sin, and a determination to turn away from it and back to Him. The affliction experienced by the Jews shows that God does not tolerate our sinful waywardness, and will take significant steps to make us 'get real' concerning the need to repent. Despite the specialness of God's people, they still had to humble themselves before Him. The necessity of repentance was a message also brought by Jesus Himself through John to the New Testament Christians in five of the seven churches addressed in Revelation (Rev 2:5,16,22; 3:3,19). In the same way, our status as God's adopted children through Jesus Christ does not nullify our need to come before Him in ongoing confession and repentance.

Seeing Jesus in the Scriptures

Jesus' ministry as recorded in the Gospels included healing the sick, raising the dead, delivering the demonised and bringing release to those in oppression – but it also involved preaching and teaching. The Gospel writers (Matthew and Mark) specified that His first words, in terms of preaching, were calls to repentance. 'From that time on Jesus began to preach, "Repent, for the kingdom of heaven has come near"' (Matt. 4:17); 'The kingdom of God has come near. Repent and believe the good news' (Mark 1:15). That specific message regarding repentance – also included in the well-known parables of the lost sheep and lost silver (Luke 15:1–10) – was distinctly mirrored in what Joel was bringing in his prophecy.

WEEK THREE

Raising the alarm

Opening Icebreaker

Compile a list of different ways warnings are given, highlighting actual (or potential) danger to property or personal safety. Discuss the steps that are taken to ensure that these warnings are as effective as possible.

Bible Readings

- Joel 2:1–11
- Numbers 10:1–9
- Psalm 19:7–11
- 1 Corinthians 10:11–15
- 1 Thessalonians 4:1–6

Opening Our Eyes

'This product contains nuts.' 'Beware of wet floor.' 'Stand on the right.' 'Shield this screen when entering your PIN.' We see warnings almost everywhere we go. While some may be given in order to avoid potential litigation, others are an insult to common sense! However, when recognised authorities such as the police or fire services display a warning then it would be foolish to ignore or discard such a message.

Two millennia ago, people also had to face hazards. These may have been very different from today, but so were the methods available to signal an alarm. Although they lacked our technology, the simple action of sounding a trumpet was the next best means of broadcasting warnings. It could alert a large number of people over a fair distance about some form of trouble lying ahead. It also shook people out of potential lethargy, telling them to wake up to reality!

Trumpets

The use of trumpets was prescribed many centuries before Joel when God gave instructions to His people through Moses. 'Make two trumpets of hammered silver, and use them for calling the community together' (Num. 10:1–2). Sounding trumpets was vital when assembling the various tribes but there were other scenarios in which trumpets were to be used, including military activity. 'When you go into battle in your own land against an enemy who is oppressing you, sound a blast on the trumpets' (Num. 10:9). Although aimed at effecting a response from God, it also served to initially raise an alarm (Jer. 4:5; 6:1; Hosea 5:8).

It was about military danger that Joel was warning God's people. 'A large and mighty army comes, such as never was in ancient times nor ever will be in ages to come' (Joel 2:2). Although this was bad enough, there were three other interwoven factors that added to the seriousness of this alarm.

Further factors

Firstly, the alarm was to be sounded in 'Zion... my holy hill' (v1), specifying Jerusalem. God's people may have believed that this location was sacred and therefore untouchable but, by naming the place of the trumpet blast, it indicated a significant act of God affecting the heart of the nation. Secondly, Joel's statement 'for the day of the Lord is coming' pinpointed God's intention of acting in a very clear and direct way. Having then described the character of the approaching 'army' (vv2–9), Joel concludes by confirming, thirdly, that it was God Himself who was in control of this coming force. 'The LORD thunders at the head of his army; his forces are beyond number, and mighty is the army that obeys his command' (v11).

The relentless nature of the 'army' indicated that this was not a recognised military force. There is no suggestion of negotiation, 'buying off' or even combating these invaders. Such action would be impossible with a horde of locusts.

But raising the alarm was also evidence of God's mercy. This invasion was not a horrific bolt from the blue. God's messages through successive prophets pointed to His concern for His people. Having the trumpet blown alerted them to the need to 'get real'.

Discussion Starters

1. In what ways do natural or man-made disasters highlight our limitations as people?

_____

_____

_____

_____

2. What is key about a warning from God as experienced by Noah (Heb. 11:7)?

_____

_____

_____

3. In what ways are God's warnings through prophets like Joel applicable to ourselves (1 Cor. 10:11–15)?

_____

_____

_____

4. What words used by Joel (Joel 2:1–2) add weight to God's warning? How do they underline the need to 'get real'?

_____

_____

_____

5. What makes a trumpet blast so effective (see 1 Cor. 15:52; 1 Thess. 4:16)?

_____

_____

_____

6. What place does warning have in church life as described by the apostle Paul (see Col. 1:28; 3:15–16; 1 Thess. 5:14)? How can warnings be made in our own church situations?

_____

_____

_____

_____

7. What particular issues was Paul warning readers about? (See Gal. 5:19–21; 1 Thess. 4:1–6; 5:14; Titus 3:10.) Why do you think he specified these ones?

_____

_____

_____

_____

8. What is the value of Scripture in terms of receiving warning (Psa. 19:7–11)? How does such warning link with the other attributes of Scripture described in Psalm 19?

_____

_____

_____

_____

Personal Application

Joel's warning describing God's intention to intervene in the lives of His people clearly shows what God is capable of doing. We are not always aware of our limitations or the implications of our actions (spiritual or otherwise). However, thanks to His compassion, God warns us, raises the alarm and shows us the need to 'get real' about our behaviour and its potential consequences. We are also warned to be on the alert about the detrimental and subtle influences of other people. The apostle Paul drew the attention of the Ephesian Christians to those 'from your own number... [who] will arise and distort the truth' (Acts 20:30).

Seeing Jesus in the Scriptures

Jesus' teaching included clear warnings about needing to have correct attitudes as well as actions. On being told about a particular atrocity involving cruel loss of life, He had replied with a warning: 'Unless you repent, you too will all perish.' Identical words were contained in His follow-up when referring to an incident (seemingly an accident) that had also seen loss of life (Luke 13:1–5). But warnings also have an implication for the future. For example, prophecies about the second coming of Jesus stress the need to be alert and watchful. There will be various 'signs' to warn, highlight and prepare us for what is to come, culminating in Christ's return (Matt. 24:4,15,32,42,44).

WEEK FOUR

Response

Opening Icebreaker

Using the internet, access a high street bank website to ascertain the steps needed to open a current account. Discuss the reasons behind the steps that need to be taken.

Bible Readings

- Joel 2:12–17
- Psalm 51
- Matthew 15:3–9
- Luke 15:11–32
- John 21:15–24

Opening Our Eyes

Three days after being appointed as prime minister, Winston Churchill made his first statement as leader to the assembled House of Commons. The year was 1940 and Britain was facing the frightening military power of a totalitarian regime. His words to parliament on that May bank holiday showed his clear response to that grim situation: 'I would say to the House, as I said to those who have joined this government, that I have nothing to offer but blood, toil, tears and sweat.' It was Churchill's amazing oratory that galvanised the country into positively responding to the threat of disaster.

Joel, the prophet, similarly used words when God's people were facing an overwhelming threat. But they were words from God which, like those words of 1940, also required a response. This response was to be shown in three ways.

1. Rending

The recurring theme of the book of Joel for God's people to 'get real' again emerges. Tearing one's clothes was commonly done at that time as a means of expressing grief. Joshua, David and Ezra were recorded as responding in this way when hearing news that greatly disturbed them. (This was, respectively, when the Israelites wanted to return to Egypt – Num. 14:6; when David learnt of his son's rebellion – 2 Sam. 13:31; and when Nehemiah was told of Jews intermarrying with non-Jews – Ezra 9:3.) God, however, did not just want an outward show from His people at this time but a genuine expression of a changed heart. The psalmist confirmed this requirement to be 'real'. 'My sacrifice, O God, is a broken spirit; a broken and contrite heart you, God, will not despise' (Psa. 51:17).

2. Remembering

Being 'real', in terms of recognising our condition before God, has an encouraging element. The prophet directs

God's people to specifically remember His graciousness and compassion. He is 'slow to anger and abounding in love' (Joel 2:13). These are repeated descriptions of God recorded in the Old Testament. Joel adds that God may not only turn away from sending the 'calamity' that was previously described, but instead may 'leave behind a blessing' (v14) following a genuine response of turning back to Him.

3. Rallying

The third aspect of this response to what God was saying involved the people being urged to come together. Joel was so moved by the threatening situation and the need for a change of heart that he directed the blowing of the trumpet in Zion, the heart of the nation (v15). This was to call the people to rally around. A public show of repentance was needed. No one was to be left out. Even the recently married, normally exempt from outside commitments, were to be included alongside those of all ages. Just as Churchill had called the people of Britain together in 1940 (two national days of prayer were subsequently held in that year), so Joel saw the need for a united response. The details were clearly described, including the key role of the priests. They were to cry out to God using the opening plea: 'Spare your people, LORD' (v17). 'Getting real' was required in order for a genuine response of fasting, consecration to God and weeping before God.

Discussion Starters

1. Why was making an outward show of returning to God not enough? What did Jesus say about such outward show (see Matt. 15:3–9)?

2. What does Psalm 51 teach us about how we should return to God?

3. How can a change of heart be revealed, as described by Joel (Joel 2:12)? How can that relate to ourselves?

4. Why is it important to be aware of God's character, in terms of His willingness to relent from sending calamity, when we turn back to Him?

5. What unstated but demonstrated characteristics did the prodigal son's father have, which drove the son to return home (see Luke 15:11–32)? How do these reflect God's character?

_____

_____

_____

_____

6. What other examples are there in the Bible of people turning back to God?

_____

_____

_____

_____

7. Joel indicated that the priests were to come to God together. What is the value of meeting together with other Christians when taking steps to return to God?

_____

_____

_____

_____

8. The priests were instructed to be specific when praying to God about their need to return to Him (Joel 2:17). Why is it important that we do the same?

_____

_____

_____

_____

Personal Application

Our need to return to God is one that is ongoing. We easily stray from Him, deliberately sin at times, slip into sin without realising it on other occasions, and are liable to get sucked back into this world's mindset and self-centred actions. 'Getting real' about distractions from our walk with God entails genuine heart response on our part, worked out in specific action indicated by Joel. This is a recurrent theme of Paul's New Testament letters. The apostle pointed out to his readers that it was down to them to ensure that, with God's help, their lives kept to God's ways: 'You were taught, with regard to your former way of life, to put off your old self... and to put on the new self' (Eph. 4:22–24).

Seeing Jesus in the Scriptures

Jesus' ministry and teaching clearly reflected those words of Joel: 'for he is gracious and compassionate' (Joel 2:13). Jesus spoke specifically of His aim 'to seek and to save the lost' (Luke 19:10), and that He had 'not come to call the righteous, but sinners' (Matt. 9:13). Similarly, the characteristic of Jesus' conversation with people around Him was highlighted: 'All spoke well of him and were amazed at the gracious words that came from his lips' (Luke 4:22). His loving intervention in Peter's situation demonstrated His desire to bring back those who had turned away from Him (see John 21:15–24).

WEEK FIVE

Restoration

Opening Icebreaker

Discuss the different ways of recycling domestic waste, and the positive spin that is used to encourage residents to actively engage in recycling.

Bible Readings

- Joel 2:18–32
- Isaiah 40:1–5
- Jeremiah 31:1–6
- Lamentations 3:19–24
- Acts 2:5–24

Opening Our Eyes

An area of land equivalent to almost 300 football pitches, heavily polluted with industrial waste, lying derelict and abandoned for years was viewed as worthless and unusable. But when London was proposed as the host city for the 2012 Summer Olympic and Paralympic Games, this patch of the East End was seen as the best location for the required sports complex. Having won the nomination for the Games, a huge amount of work was undertaken to clear the site including removal of radioactive waste and other toxic materials. Subsequent regeneration projects on the site, including housing and community facilities, continued to be constructed once the Games were over.

Spiritual neglect and pollution from surrounding influences, together with an unwillingness to 'get real' had had a devastating effect on God's people. But the prophet Joel, having drawn attention to the need to repent and respond to God, now changes the tone of his message. He describes what God is in the process of doing: taking pity on a hopeless and seemingly unchangeable scenario (Joel 2:18). In describing God's intervention, Joel was drawing the people's attention to three aspects about which they needed to 'get real'.

1. Recognisable
'I am sending you grain, new wine and olive oil, enough to satisfy you fully' (Joel 2:19). Joel describes God's provision for His people in very recognisable ways: rainfall, large harvests and plentiful produce (vv22–24). But these were just the obvious displays of God's care and affirmation. His people needed to be aware that He had 'pity' on them, did not want them to be 'afraid' but rather to be 'glad' and to 'rejoice in the LORD your God' (vv18,21,23). God was not just offering physical satisfaction, but an inner and deep seated sense of peace.

2. Regeneration

'I will drive the northern horde far from you' (Joel 2:20). Secondly, God's saving power, in contrast to His people's abject powerlessness, was to be seen in the summary removal of the horde of locusts. But, again, there was a significance lying behind this physical action. The shame, stigma and hopelessness that this invasion had generated was also to be removed (vv19,26,27). This included God's power being exercised so that He would 'repay them for the years the locusts have eaten' (v25). God's 'regeneration programme' is far in excess of what humankind can achieve! Joel underlines this quality of God: 'Surely the LORD has done great things!' (v21).

3. Release

'I will pour out my Spirit on all people' (Joel 2:28). Finally, the physical and emotional provision of God described above culminates in this description of His awesome plan to release His Spirit on 'all flesh' (v28, KJV). It's as though God can no longer restrain Himself. He has removed the restriction of His Spirit solely coming upon certain people for specific high profile roles. People from *all* strata of society and all nations (not just Jews) will experience God's powerful intervention in this way. The climatic signs of the outpouring of God's Spirit will point to the return of Jesus Christ, 'the coming of the great and dreadful day of the LORD' (vv30–31). Joel records God's mercy being shown in that people were able to return to Him even in those awesome times.

Discussion Starters

1. Why is it important to understand God's pity and compassion as described by Old Testament writers (Isa. 40:1–5; Jer. 31:1–6; Lam. 3:19–24)?

2. Why was God's pity towards His people shown in earthly fruitfulness and abundance (Joel 2:19,22–26)? What does this mean for us today?

3. In what ways did God's action of driving away the locusts reflect His character? How does this relate to us?

4. What does Joel say about the ways God wanted His people to respond to these 'great things' that He was doing? How did this response show that His people were 'getting real' about their transformed situation?

5. In what ways was God repaying His people for the years that 'the locusts have eaten' (Joel 2:25)?

_____

_____

_____

_____

6. What were the qualities of God, as described in Lamentations, that changed the writer's perception and enabled him to 'get real' (Lam. 3:19–24)?

_____

_____

_____

_____

7. What were the promises of God regarding the release of His Spirit that Peter wanted to highlight (Joel 2:28–29; Acts 2:5–24)?

_____

_____

_____

_____

8. Why was it important that details of those 'signs' and 'wonders' be included in this description of the release of the Spirit (Acts 2:17–21)?

_____

_____

_____

_____

Personal Application

'Getting real' with God not only involves seeing our need to repent and respond to God, but recognising His power to transform situations that are entirely out of our hands. This may involve material provision but, more importantly, a sense of inner satisfaction and peace. John recorded that 'God gives the Spirit without limit' (John 3:34) and Paul urged his readers to 'be filled with the Spirit' (Eph. 5:18). The Old Testament frequently highlights the need to 'get real' by pointing out God's wonderful works. These involve physical and spiritual blessings that demand our response, as written in the Psalms: 'Praise the LORD, my soul, and forget not all his benefits' (Psa. 103:2).

Seeing Jesus in the Scriptures

The work of Jesus in bringing salvation to His people, those who call 'on the name of the LORD' (Joel 2:32), is more clearly identified at the close of this passage. It points to the physical location of that salvation ('on Mount Zion and in Jerusalem', v32) where Jesus was crucified, as well as being the ultimate demonstration of God's compassion and power. It was this passage from Joel's prophecy that Peter quoted in his sermon on the day of Pentecost. He used it as a powerful means of underlining what his hearers needed to recognise and experience. Jesus of Nazareth was the Christ, resurrected from the dead, exalted to the right hand of God, and who had now clearly poured out the promised Holy Spirit.

WEEK SIX

Retribution

Opening Icebreaker

Discuss different examination methods for determining whether students have passed or failed in a particular subject. Consider why these different methods are used.

Bible Readings

- Joel 3:1–16
- Matthew 25:31–46
- 1 Peter 1:1–2; 2:9
- 2 Peter 3:1–18
- Revelation 1:9–20

Opening Our Eyes

'You won't get away with this' are words that have been uttered by victims in films and crime-based novels. They may have been met with a disdainful sneer by the 'baddie' but justice is ultimately seen to prevail. But such scenarios where wrongs are put right also arise in real life. Simon Wiesenthal was a Jew who worked hard to bring to account some of those responsible for the Holocaust of the Second World War. Sometimes this was achieved only after many years of extremely painstaking work in tracking down these war criminals.

For most people, there is a sense that perpetrators of wrongful acts should not be allowed to get away with it. It is in that context that Joel closes his prophecy by describing the action to be taken in respect of those who had abused and subjugated God's people. He had previously stressed the need for his compatriots to 'get real.' Now that sentiment is directed at those oppressive nations. They needed to 'get real' because God's retribution was heading their way. Five aspects are highlighted in this ultimate 'examination' of nations.

1. Place
Joel says that God will 'gather all nations and bring them down to the Valley of Jehoshaphat' (Joel 3:2). Although this location is not specified anywhere else in Scripture, it pointed to the fact that no nation would avoid or escape God's scrutiny.

2. Purpose
The reason for the nations being gathered was for them to be put 'on trial' (v2). The Valley of Jehoshaphat would be a place of 'decision' (v14). God would judge on the actions of each nation 'for what they did to my inheritance, my people Israel' (v2).

3. Perpetration

God's examination includes what might be described as a charge-sheet. The evils perpetrated by nations are listed: 'because they scattered my people among the nations and divided up my land. They cast lots for my people and traded boys for prostitutes; they sold girls for wine to drink' (Joel 3:2–3). Other crimes against God's people included pillaging and enslavement. God was also clearly 'naming names' (Tyre, Sidon, Philistia – v4).

4. Punishment

Two pictures are presented in respect of God's retribution against those who oppressed His people. The first is that they would experience the same affliction that they themselves had meted out to God's people (Joel 3:7–8). The second is that they would suffer the 'swing [of] the sickle' and trampling of the grapes (v13). In a somewhat unclear narrative, it seems that the latter takes place subsequent to a confrontation with the oppressors that God had summoned (Joel 3:9–11). This reflected God's intervention at the end of time (Rev. 14:14–15; 16:13–16).

5. Power

In the midst of this judgment, the awesome power of God is described: 'The sun and moon will be darkened, and the stars no longer shine... the earth and the heavens will tremble' (Joel 3:15–16). God's people are prompted to 'get real' regarding His ability to bring judgment, but are also reminded that He will be a 'refuge' and 'stronghold for the people of Israel' (v16).

Discussion Starters

1. Why is contemporary society dismissive of any concept of judgment being undertaken by God? What is Peter's response (2 Pet. 3:1–10)?

2. What should be our response to God's pending judgment (see 2 Pet. 3:11–15)?

3. What is Peter's warning to his readers in the context of God's pending judgment? How does that apply to us (2 Pet. 3:17–18)?

4. What is Joel's purpose in repeatedly using the word 'my' in Joel 3:2–3? How does this link with the subsequent judgment?

5. What is the significance of God describing His people Israel as 'my inheritance' (Joel 3:2)? How is a similar description by Peter important for ourselves (1 Pet. 2:9; 1:1–2)?

_____

_____

_____

6. In what ways does the opening verse (Joel 3:1) bring encouragement (before Joel speaks of God's retributive action)?

_____

_____

_____

7. How does God's punishment of Tyre, Sidon and Philistia reciprocate what they had done against His people (Joel 3:4–8)? What other Old Testament examples show this?

_____

_____

_____

8. What are the parallels between this section of Joel (3:1–6) and Jesus' teaching describing events relating to His second coming (Matt. 25:31–46)?

_____

_____

_____

Personal Application

The issue of God's judgment is often given little thought even by Christians. But God speaks, through His Word, of this future and certain event. As the apostle Peter emphasises, this prospect should drive us to 'get real' and conduct ourselves in a way that means we are holy and blameless (2 Pet. 3:11–12). Peter explains that God's people will experience God in this way: 'For it is time for judgment to begin with God's household; and if it begins with us, what will the outcome be for those who do not obey the gospel of God?' (1 Pet. 4:17). Paul clarifies that this 'judgment' in respect of believers relates to God's action of bringing discipline (1 Cor. 11:32). This was particularly the case for the Jews when suffering devastation at the time of Joel.

Seeing Jesus in the Scriptures

The future judgment of all people of the world, indicated by Joel in terms of what God was doing at that time, will be undertaken by the Lord Jesus Christ Himself (see Acts 17:31; 10:42–43; Matt. 25:31). This may be a shock to many, including Christians, but the Old Testament specified that Jesus would be 'given authority, glory and sovereign power' (Dan. 7:11–14). The judgment that Jesus would bring is also prefigured in the specific words of stern rebuke and serious consequences that the seven churches might have to face (Rev. 2–3).

WEEK SEVEN

Refocusing

Opening Icebreaker

Discuss how the many media outlets can affect our outlook on life. What are the different degrees of impact that they can have on us?

Bible Readings

- Joel 3:17–21
- Psalm 31:1–5
- Psalm 42
- Psalm 139:7–12
- Ephesians 2:1–10
- Colossians 2:13–15

Opening Our Eyes

A major railway station is a good place to observe crowds of people in transit and speculate on what they are anticipating at the end of their travels. Of course, if you are rushing to catch a train yourself then such surveillance is tricky. But watching travellers moving around the concourse can be interesting. Some, pushing heavy luggage on a trolley, may be on their way to an airport to face a gruelling long-haul journey abroad. Others, wheeling a smaller suitcase, might be looking forward to a short break away. Those with phones glued to their ears in concentrated conversation are probably heading for a demanding work environment, while those shepherding children might be relieved to be returning home. One place but many different outlooks and emotions.

So when God spoke to His people – also in transit – through Joel, telling them about the blessings that He was going to give them, their attitude needed to be considerably refocused. Divine messages about repentance and warnings of forthcoming invasion and judgment were followed by something very different, which required their full attention. It involved seeing God's intervention in their lives in new ways.

Refuge

Tagged at the end of previous words of condemnation and judgment against those who had opposed God's people was a statement: 'But the LORD will be a refuge… a stronghold for the people of Israel' (Joel 3:16). The original Hebrew word for 'refuge' not only related to a sheltering and protective element but also pointed to a place of hope. This was especially applicable for Joel's audience. It was underlining God's earlier message of restoration arising from 'the years the locusts have eaten' (Joel 2:25).

Reassurance

This message of hope was linked to an element of reassurance. God was wanting His people to remember that He was with them. 'I, the LORD your God, dwell in Zion, my holy hill' (Joel 3:17). This was repeated at the end of Joel's prophecy: 'The LORD dwells in Zion' (v21). It was also picked up by Matthew right at the beginning of his Gospel with reference to Jesus the Messiah: '"they will call him Immanuel" (which means "God with us")' (Matt. 1:23).

Refreshing

God further wanted His people to know that He would be bringing them the blessing of refreshment. (This was in contrast to the stripping away of everything by the locust plague.) The imagery of 'new wine,' 'milk' and 'water' all point to reinvigoration and ongoing provision (Joel 3:18). Again there is the element of subsequent repetition to confirm God's intention. 'A fountain will flow out of the LORD's house and will water the valley of acacias' (v18). What God had originally intended for His people, when entering the Promised Land ('a land flowing with milk and honey' – Num. 14:8), was now going to happen.

Release

God's blessing wasn't good news for everyone. The Israelites' enemies, specified here as constituting Egypt and Edom, would be rendered 'desolate' and a 'desert waste' (Joel 3:19), meaning that God's people would no longer have to fear an enemy invasion.

These different expressions of God's blessings needed to be clearly described so that His people could 'get real' with what He was doing. They were to refocus on the unchangeable character and purposes of God shown by picturing Judah as being inhabited 'for ever' by His people (v20). This is seen by many as prefiguring the time of Christ's return to this world as King, an event to which we are also looking forward and about which we need to 'get real'.

Discussion Starters

1. Why was it important for God's people, at the time of Joel, to 'get real' about God being present with them?

2. What assurance of God's presence at all times and in all places is described by the psalmist (Psa. 139:7–12)?

3. What different aspects of God being a 'refuge' are brought out by the psalmist (Psa. 31:1–5)?

4. Why was it particularly necessary for God's people to receive His refreshing by way of the provision of wine, milk and water? How can that relate to us?

5. How does the psalmist describe his need for God to bring him refreshment? What action does he take to experience this (see Psa. 42)?

_____

_____

_____

_____

6. What steps can we take in order to be in a place of knowing God's refreshing?

_____

_____

_____

_____

7. What does the apostle Paul tell us about the spiritual freedom that Jesus Christ has achieved for us (Col. 2:13–15)?

_____

_____

_____

_____

8. What are the blessings that we have received, through Jesus Christ and His death on the cross, regarding our new freedom (Eph. 2:1–10)?

_____

_____

_____

_____

Personal Application

We too easily lose sight of the amazing blessings that come from God, both material and spiritual. Our outlook is considerably influenced, if not dominated, by what the world says and thinks. These closing verses of Joel's prophecy are a reminder to 'get real' with what God has done for us. The psalmist was another writer in the Bible who was often reminding his readers, and himself, about the wonders of God and His provision. Psalm 103 is a good source in helping us refocus on God and His goodness. The apostle Paul complements the psalmist by underlining the superlative spiritual blessings that we have from God through Jesus Christ (Eph. 3:14–21).

Seeing Jesus in the Scriptures

The expression used by Joel regarding the provision of water ('A fountain will flow out of the LORD's house' – Joel 3:18) is a reminder of the words of Jesus concerning Himself. 'Let anyone who is thirsty come to me and drink. Whoever believes in me, as Scripture has said, rivers of living water will flow from within them' (John 7:37–38). The soul-refreshing life, which comes from coming to Christ ('getting real' about our spiritual state and need of Him) was also shared with the woman at the well in Samaria (John 4:1–26). Whatever our past experience, Jesus is the one to whom we can always come and receive 'the water I give them' (John 4:14).

Leader's Notes

Week One: Realisation

Opening Icebreaker
The main aim of newspaper headlines is to capture the attention of potential readers with words (the fewer the better) in emboldened print. The accuracy of such wording is not seen as important as its jolting effect, drawing people to want to read the report that follows.

Aim of the Session
To understand that God is involved in the affairs of this world and can use events to prompt people to 'get real' about what He wants to say to them.

Discussion Starters
1. The locust swarm caused total devastation with everything being consumed; vines and fig trees were laid waste and fields of crops were ruined. The detail was necessary so that the people would be under no illusion as to the catastrophe they were facing.

2. The locust swarm was likened to an invading army in order to underline both the size and ferocity of the swarm. Like a powerful army, the insects could not be controlled, beaten back or be engaged in negotiation as a means of reducing the carnage being sustained. This is basically the same situation when any natural disaster is being experienced.

3. Joel's hearers were instructed to weep, wail, wake up and mourn. This was to indicate a response that was deeply felt – not superficial or temporary. It was also to indicate a realisation that God was speaking to them through these events.

4. Joel initially addressed the elders because they had not prevented behaviour which had resulted in this 'invasion'. Contemporary church leadership still has the role of providing sound teaching, active pastoring and good role-modelling for those under their spiritual care.

5. Other biblical disasters sent by God include the affliction of plague, drought, famine, blight, mildew, locusts, darkness, pollution and infestation. The ten plagues inflicted upon the Egyptians at the time of Moses (Psa. 105; Exod. 7–11) are a notable example of God's intervention. This was to enable His people to escape from slavery.

6. Natural disasters – sometimes termed 'acts of God' – are generally unpredictable and uncontrollable with no one person (or group of people) to blame or be held responsible. Other than a generalised comment that global warming might be a factor, our reaction is simply to accept what has happened and to take action to help victims. Our reaction to man-made disasters is often to demand someone being identified as responsible for what has occurred.

7. God's people, at the time of Joel, were self-centred, distant from God and unaware that He might be intervening in some way. Today, there is a sophisticated belief that science and technology rules out any idea that God can supernaturally be involved in the affairs of the world.

8. We can be more alert to the ways in which God intervenes through reading biblical narratives and also by hearing and reading about testimonies and experiences of Christians, past and present.

Week Two: Repentance

Opening Icebreaker
Questions are asked in order to ascertain the exact nature and root of the problem (not just the symptoms). Only then can enquiries be made about how things might be resolved or those symptoms mitigated. Further questions might arise in terms of asking for help and advice.

Aim of the Session
To understand the need for us to come to God in genuine repentance, and the steps God takes in order to get us to that point.

Discussion Starters
1. The priests held particular spiritual authority in what was (or was not) taking place. They needed to be specifically told how God viewed the state of His people, and to take a lead (showing an example) in the response that God required by way of repentance. Although neither was actually a priest, both Nehemiah and Daniel grasped this aspect of responsibility and example (see Neh. 1:4, Dan. 9:3).

2. God wanted specific and definite action to be undertaken, both privately at night and publicly in the daytime. This was a means of showing obedience to His direction and genuine repentance for the spiritual condition of His people. In a similar way, we are also called by God to take deliberate steps to confess and repent of sin, as shown in 1 John 1:8–9.

3. Attention was drawn back to the effects of the locust swarm so that God's people had no doubt how He viewed their spiritual state and waywardness. The devastation they had suffered had been allowed by God as a means of making them 'get real' regarding their sin.

4. Joel and the elders were to acknowledge their failure, confess their sin and admit that He had not been obeyed. They also needed to face up to the fact that God's action, in bringing devastation, had been in accordance to what He had previously warned through the law of Moses.

5. Despite the evil actions of people (particularly of King Ahab), God responds to genuine and clear repentance. In both cases, God did not bring judgment, previously described by Elijah and Jonah, on the king or people of Nineveh.

6. John the Baptist preached about the need for repentance, with confession leading to baptism. Elsewhere, he gave specific instructions regarding what repentance was to entail (Luke 3:7–14). Joel also brought precise details as to how turning to God was to be shown in an outward sense.

7. Jesus validated John's call to repentance by being baptised Himself, and by preaching about it (Luke 5:32; 15:7; 15:10).

8. The Church should still be emphasising the seriousness of sin and turning from God's ways. This needs to be done through teaching about the necessity to come back to God with an attitude of genuine and humble repentance, as stressed in Peter's sermons (Acts 2:38,40; 3:19).

Week Three: Raising the alarm

Opening Icebreaker
Many contemporary alarm systems combine an audible and visual element. Sirens, klaxons, bleeps or recorded voices are all designed to attract attention and point to action. Flashing lights and clear signage may also feature. The noisier, brighter and more obvious the alert, the better!

Aim of the Session
To understand that God brings clear and direct warnings regarding wrong action that we may be about to make, or have already made.

Discussion Starters
1. Natural disasters, especially when striking without warning, particularly highlight the fragility of life and its brevity. They point to the fact that humankind does not have as much control as may be assumed, and that huge changes can occur in milliseconds even to the extent of lives suddenly being lost. Man-made catastrophes also warn us about the limitations of our knowledge and expertise, which can result in failures and unexpected situations arising.

2. What is key about God's warnings is that they are about dangers 'not yet seen' (Heb. 11:7). God's people, at the time of Joel, were not aware of what possibly constituted a further wave or an increased intensity of approaching locusts, which was why the warning was made. Similarly, like Noah, we may be ignorant of pending dangers arising from God's judgment or discipline unless we are warned by God. Paul warned the Thessalonian church about rejecting instructions that he'd previously given (1 Thess. 4:2,8), perhaps because they had not expected any consequences.

3. The apostle Paul explains that the judgment and discipline exacted on the children of Israel by God, when in the wilderness, was to be seen as a particular warning to ourselves. This is particularly the case where there is the sense of self-sufficiency and presumption that there's nothing wrong. The written nature of that warning indicates the seriousness of what is being stated.

4. The specific phrase 'close at hand' (Joel 2:1) emphasises the clear, definite and awesome action that God is about to take. It is obvious that God will not deviate from His decision to act and this warning therefore demands that the hearers 'get real' about responding.

5. A trumpet blast is loud, can carry its sound over a large area and is not dependent on the limitations of the human voice. It is also clear and distinctive, strident in its sound thus demanding attention.

6. Paul saw the need for warning to take place alongside encouragement and teaching. It is designed to address specific failings and issues. Warnings may be viewed as being an integral part of discipline. In that context, a general warning is initially given (particularly in the context of preaching and teaching) followed up in a pastoral or counselling scenario if there is no clear response (see 2 Tim. 4:1–2).

7. The issues that Paul was warning his readers about included idolatry, idleness, quarrelling, divisiveness and immorality. They may not have seemed particularly serious, especially in those days, but Paul was alerting the Christians to the need to 'get real' as to how God saw such behaviour, and to deal thoroughly with it.

8. Because the Bible is written down for us to read it means that we can access what God is saying (including His warnings) at any time or place. The ability of Scripture to refresh the soul and make wise the simple (Psa. 19:7) are greatly beneficial and shows that although warnings may seem to be negative, they are aimed as being from God for our spiritual good.

Week Four: Response

Opening Icebreaker
The steps needed to open a bank account involve appropriate and correct responses to questions, shown on the screen, to do with identity details of the applicant, employment, house ownership and financial status. Only after valid answers are given is there access to the next stage.

Aim of the Session
To show that God requires appropriate responses to what He says, especially His warnings.

Discussion Starters
1. For God, an outward show of repentance was not an adequate response. Going through the motions is superficial and unreal. Jesus described such action as hypocrisy on the part of people whose hearts were actually far from God.

2. The psalmist describes the need for humility before God, recognising our depraved condition and turning to Him as one who is totally just. We need to turn away from sin and rebellion. There is also the need to understand that only God can deal with sin and make us clean.

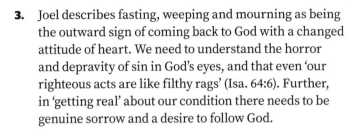

3. Joel describes fasting, weeping and mourning as being the outward sign of coming back to God with a changed attitude of heart. We need to understand the horror and depravity of sin in God's eyes, and that even 'our righteous acts are like filthy rags' (Isa. 64:6). Further, in 'getting real' about our condition there needs to be genuine sorrow and a desire to follow God.

4. Being reminded of God's grace and compassion, together with His willingness to relent from sending calamity, is an encouragement to 'get real' about our situation. It means that we are aware of God's attitude towards us when turning back to Him.

5. The son recognised that his father treated his servants well by feeding and looking after them. When the son returned home, his father's love was clearly demonstrated in the fact that he was looking out for his son and ran to greet him when even 'a long way off' (Luke 15:20). Jesus' parable about the lost son (following that of the lost silver and sheep) aimed to show God's unconditional acceptance towards, and rejoicing about, those who were 'lost' now being 'found'.

6. Other examples of people turning back to God include Peter (John 21:15–24), David (2 Sam. 12; Psa. 51) and Jonah (Jonah 2–3).

7. Meeting with other Christians is a means of receiving encouragement and spiritually building up each other (Heb. 10:25; 1 Thess. 5:11). It also means obeying God's command to be with other believers and where Jesus has promised to be present (Matt. 18:20).

8. Being specific and verbalising our needs is a way of 'getting real' with ourselves and with God. Highlighting our condition, including our helplessness and desperate situation (as those priests were directed to describe) confirms our dependence upon God alone. The psalmist was particularly 'real' about his situations when coming to God (see Psa. 13; 25; 142; 143).

Week Five: Restoration

Opening Icebreaker
Methods of recycling might include weekly or regular collection of sorted waste from domestic properties, central collecting centres, collection of unwanted items in designated charity plastic bags, and donation of items to charity shops. Benefits might include unwanted items being of value to other people, being reprocessed to produce useful material or goods, and utilising materials that would otherwise occupy landfill sites. There is a general sense of discarded stuff being restored to have value and purpose.

Aim of the Session
To understand that God sees us as having worth and value, and that He is able to bring transformation to our messed up lives thereby giving us hope.

Discussion Starters
1. As these Old Testament writers indicate, we (and God's people of Joel's time) can be so overwhelmed by sin and failure that we forget God's mercy and compassion. We might have a deep sense of worthlessness and hopelessness that only a revelation of God's love can change.

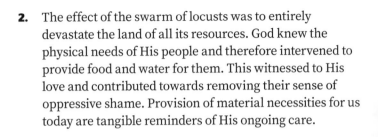

2. The effect of the swarm of locusts was to entirely devastate the land of all its resources. God knew the physical needs of His people and therefore intervened to provide food and water for them. This witnessed to His love and contributed towards removing their sense of oppressive shame. Provision of material necessities for us today are tangible reminders of His ongoing care.

3. God driving away the locusts showed His absolute power against a force, which His people were helpless to counteract. It also showed that He was able to bring them to a state of mind whereby they did not need to fear. We also need to be aware of God's restorative power and love when having to contend with whatever physical or spiritual forces may confront us. It means that we can be assured that He gives us 'hope and a future' (Jer. 29:11).

4. God wanted His people to 'be glad and rejoice' (Joel 2:21), not to be afraid (v22) and to 'praise the name of the LORD your God' (v26). This would show their recognition of Him alone being able to transform their physical and spiritual situation.

5. God was providing an abundance of food (Joel 2:26) and giving back hope (v27), both of which had been lost as a consequence of the locusts. It was important that God's people be aware of the fact that He was acting in these ways so that their past experiences could be put behind them and they could be confident about their future being in God's care.

6. A similar scenario was being experienced by the writer of Lamentations when the country was facing invasion from a relentless oppressor. He was brought to realise that he needed to focus on God's love and compassion that would never fail and are 'new every morning' (Lam 3:23).

7. Peter wanted to stress that the outpouring of God's Spirit at Pentecost was a fulfilment of Joel's prophecy and that all peoples and nations would be able to experience God in this way. The cross-section of the world's population gathered at Jerusalem were subsequently the recipients of this outpouring as Peter then explained: 'The promise is for you and your children and for all who are far off – for all whom the Lord our God will call' (Acts 2:39).

8. The signs and wonders highlighted the holiness and power of God, about which people needed to 'get real', responding to Him in the right way and calling on Him for salvation.

Week Six: Retribution

Opening Icebreaker
Exams are likely to consist of written or oral questions needing written or oral answers, project portfolios being produced following a set period of research, practical assessment and demonstration of competencies. These are all designed to assess knowledge, ability, application and judgment both in a controlled environment and a 'hands on' setting.

Aim of the Session
To understand that God is one who is also the judge and will bring judgment upon people for their attitude towards Him.

Discussion Starters
1. The main reason why people are dismissive of judgment from or by God is that they cannot see any indication of such action being carried out. People are so absorbed in their own lifestyles that there is no space for God or perception of His pending action. Peter describes them as 'scoffers' (2 Pet. 3:3).

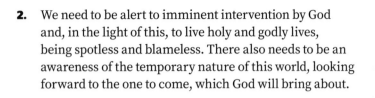

2. We need to be alert to imminent intervention by God and, in the light of this, to live holy and godly lives, being spotless and blameless. There also needs to be an awareness of the temporary nature of this world, looking forward to the one to come, which God will bring about.

3. We need to 'get real' about God's intention to bring judgment, and not turn away from God through taking on board the attitudes and actions of the ungodly (2 Pet. 3:17). Not even the angels were spared when some of them rebelled. God also needed to act in order to rescue Lot from a godless and depraved environment (2 Pet. 2:4–9).

4. Joel's use of the word 'my' shows God's relationship with His people. The judgment described in the following verses is not just because of what the nations have done against Israel, but the way that they have actually acted against God Himself.

5. The use of the word 'inheritance' (Joel 3:2) points to the very special place that Israel holds in God's eyes, their value to Him and the security they have as a consequence. Peter takes this further in describing Christians as being seen by God in the same way and that we are 'shielded by God's power' (1 Pet. 1:5).

6. The words used by Joel indicate the sovereign power and authority of God. His intention to act at a particular time and bring restoration will not be thwarted. He is aware of His people's plight and helplessness. We can similarly draw assurance from God's willingness and ability to protect us (as previously indicated in 1 Pet. 1:3–5).

7. God's justice is seen in meting out to those people groups what they had themselves inflicted upon Israel. His retribution is described as being completely just (Gen. 18:25; Deut. 32:4). Examples include: Pharaoh being punished for carrying out infanticide against Hebrew babies by losing his firstborn to God's angel of death at the Passover; and Haman being hung on the gallows he'd prepared for Mordecai.

8. Both passages from Joel and Matthew clearly describe God's judgment upon people based on their actions and attitudes against His people: 'brothers and sisters of mine' (Matt. 25:40).

Week Seven: Refocusing

Opening Icebreaker
Television, the internet and social media have particularly strong influences on people's outlook and focus. Social media, involving interaction and input – immediate and widespread – is especially powerful in this respect. Other media sources such as newspapers provide data and opinion but don't enable the same level of immediate response.

Aim of the Session
To highlight that God needs to be our sole focus in life. He alone provides for our real needs.

Discussion Starters
1. God's people had experienced significant traumatic oppression by way of swarms of locusts devastating their crops and livelihoods, and the incursion of their enemies. This would not only have had physical but also negative emotional and spiritual impact. They needed to be made aware that God had not abandoned them or regarded them as a hopeless case.

2. The psalmist reminds himself – and us – of the fact that wherever he goes or however far the journey, God is always with him, whatever the time. Not only that, but God's hand is guarding and guiding him, holding him 'fast' (Psa. 139:10).

3. Two powerful images are presented in Psalm 31 of God being a 'refuge' (v1): 'rock of refuge' (v2) and 'strong fortress' (v2). These mean that God is the one who listens, rescues, saves, gives guidance and brings deliverance and freedom.

4. God's people had gone through times of sustained and oppressive hardship, being unable to effect any change or relief by means of their own resources. This provision by God was essential for their recovery not only at a physical level but also in focusing on His spiritual refreshment.

5. The psalmist likens his need to that of a deer needing water for refreshment. He knew that his spiritual thirst could only be satisfied by focusing on God. This is done by acknowledging his need of God (42:1–4), 'getting real' with himself about his spiritual condition (vv5–6), calling out to God (vv7–8), telling God of his condition (vv9–10) and expressing his trust in God to lift him up as he focuses on Him (v11).

6. Similar to the psalmist in Psalm 42, we need to 'get real' about our condition, focus on God and acknowledge Him as being the only source of refreshment.

7. Paul describes our condition as that of being spiritually 'dead', being charged with 'legal indebtedness', being 'condemned' and oppressed by 'the powers and authorities'. Like God's people at the time of Joel, there

is no way that we can change our condition or effect release. That is only achieved through the work of Jesus. Through His death on the cross, the charge against us is 'cancelled' and 'taken away'. Jesus triumphs over those spiritual forces against us, which are 'disarmed' and made a 'public spectacle... by the cross' (Col. 2:13–15).

8. In Ephesians, Paul again sets out our spiritual condition. We are 'dead'. We have 'followed the ways of this world', having our focus on 'gratifying the cravings of our flesh'. He then calls us to refocus on the love of God shown through the work of Christ, achieving for us what we could not do for ourselves. This leads us to realise that, like those of Joel's time, we are 'God's handiwork' created to do 'good works... prepared in advance for us to do' (Eph. 2:1–10). As with God's people of the Old and New Testaments, we need to 'get real' about how God sees us, what He has done for us, and the future that He plans for us.

Notes...

The *Cover to Cover* Bible Study Series

1 Corinthians
Growing a Spirit-filled church
ISBN: 978-1-85345-374-8

2 Corinthians
Restoring harmony
ISBN: 978-1-85345-551-3

1,2,3 John
Walking in the truth
ISBN: 978-1-78259-763-6

1 Peter
Good reasons for hope
ISBN: 978-1-78259-088-0

2 Peter
Living in the light of God's
promises
ISBN: 978-1-78259-403-1

23rd Psalm
The Lord is my shepherd
ISBN: 978-1-85345-449-3

1 Timothy
Healthy churches – effective
Christians
ISBN: 978-1-85345-291-8

2 Timothy and Titus
Vital Christianity
ISBN: 978-1-85345-338-0

Abraham
Adventures of faith
ISBN: 978-1-78259-089-7

Acts 1–12
Church on the move
ISBN: 978-1-85345-574-2

Acts 13–28
To the ends of the earth
ISBN: 978-1-85345-592-6

Barnabas
Son of encouragement
ISBN: 978-1-85345-911-5

Bible Genres
Hearing what the Bible really says
ISBN: 978-1-85345-987-0

Daniel
Living boldly for God
ISBN: 978-1-85345-986-3

David
A man after God's own heart
ISBN: 978-1-78259-444-4

Ecclesiastes
Hard questions and spiritual
answers
ISBN: 978-1-85345-371-7

Elijah
A man and his God
ISBN: 978-1-85345-575-9

Elisha
A lesson in faithfulness
ISBN: 978-1-78259-494-9

Ephesians
Claiming your inheritance
ISBN: 978-1-85345-229-1

Esther
For such a time as this
ISBN: 978-1-85345-511-7

Ezekiel
A prophet for all times
ISBN: 978-1-78259-836-7

Fruit of the Spirit
Growing more like Jesus
ISBN: 978-1-85345-375-5

Galatians
Freedom in Christ
ISBN: 978-1-85345-648-0

Genesis 1–11
Foundations of reality
ISBN: 978-1-85345-404-2

Genesis 12–50
Founding fathers of faith
ISBN: 978-1-78259-960-9

God's Rescue Plan
Finding God's fingerprints on
human history
ISBN: 978-1-85345-294-9

Great Prayers of the Bible
Applying them to our lives toda
ISBN: 978-1-85345-253-6

Habakkuk
Choosing God's way
ISBN: 978-1-78259-843-5

Haggai
Motivating God's people
ISBN: 978-1-78259-686-8

Hebrews
Jesus – simply the best
ISBN: 978-1-85345-337-3

Isaiah 1–39
Prophet to the nations
ISBN: 978-1-85345-510-0

Isaiah 40–66
Prophet of restoration
ISBN: 978-1-85345-550-6

For current prices or to order, visit **cwr.org.uk/shop**
Available online or from Christian bookshops.

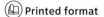 

SmallGroup central

All of our small group ideas and resources in one place

Online:

smallgroupcentral.org.uk
is filled with free video teaching, tools, articles and a whole host of ideas.

On the road:

A range of seminars themed for small groups can be brought to your local community. Contact us at *hello@smallgroupcentral.org.uk*

In print:

Books, study guides and DVDs covering an extensive list of themes, Bible books and life issues.

Find out more at:
smallgroupcentral.org.uk

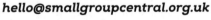

Courses and events

Waverley Abbey College

Publishing and media

Conference facilities

Transforming lives

CWR's vision is to enable people to experience personal transformation through applying God's Word to their lives and relationships.

Our Bible-based training and resources help people around the world to:
• Grow in their walk with God
• Understand and apply Scripture to their lives
• Resource themselves and their church
• Develop pastoral care and counselling skills
• Train for leadership
• Strengthen relationships, marriage and family life and much more.

CWR Applying God's Word
to everyday life and relationships

CWR, Waverley Abbey House,
Waverley Lane, Farnham,
Surrey GU9 8EP, UK

Telephone: **+44 (0)1252 784700**
Email: **info@cwr.org.uk**
Website: **cwr.org.uk**

Registered Charity No. 294387
Company Registration No. 1990308

Our insightful writers provide daily Bible reading notes and other resources for all ages, and our experienced course designers and presenters have gained an international reputation for excellence and effectiveness.

CWR's Training and Conference Centre in Surrey, England, provides excellent facilities in an idyllic setting – ideal for both learning and spiritual refreshment.